THE CLASSICAL ERA

An Introduction to the Keyboard Music

Edited by
Willard A. Palmer & Margery Halford

CONTENTS

THE CLASSICAL ERA

Elegance
Restraint
Grace
Clarity
Balance
Contrast
Symmetry

The graceful, balanced symmetry of classical architecture is seen in the *Brandenburg Gate,* Berlin, built 1788-91.

These words describe the tendencies of the architecture, the art, and the music of the classical era – the period that began around 1750 and continued into the early 1800s.

It was to be expected that the freely decorated, elaborate style of the baroque era should eventually give way to a more restrained and formal approach in all the arts. The beauty of the ancient Greek and Roman temples, many of which were newly excavated during these years, was seen as an ideal form of architecture.

The balance, symmetry, and strong contrasts of geometrical shapes with subtle decorations were considered to be more tasteful than the excessively ornate, rococo structures popular in the baroque era.

In music, the elaborated single *motive* or *idea* of baroque composition began to give way to longer themes, several of which were used in contrast in the same movement. Form became a primary factor in compostion, resulting in a musical structure as balanced and symmetrical as a temple.

ABOUT THIS BOOK

This book discusses the style and development of keyboard music of the classical period. It begins with those composers whose works contributed most noticeably to the development of the classical forms and who are often called *pre-classical.* Among these are Leopold Mozart, the sons of J.S. Bach, Domenico Alberti, and Georg Christoph Wagenseil. At the end of the baroque period, the most popular form of keyboard composition was the *suite*, composed principally of a series of dance movements (*Allemandes, Courantes, Sarabandes, Menuets, Gigues,* etc.). Of these movements, the *Menuet & Trio,* with its balanced and contrasting sections, was most compatible with the classical ideal. It was one of the few dance forms that remained popular throughout the classical period and became a part of the most important classical form, the three or four movement *sonata.* The development of the classical sonata is discussed on the following pages. The book continues with examples from the works of the greatest classical composers, Haydn, Mozart, and Clementi, ending with Beethoven, who brought to classical music many innovations, and whose later works mark the beginning of the romantic movement that followed.

Classicism in Architecture, Art & Music

The pictures in this book present the eye with restrained elegance and balanced grace that appear so natural and unforced that nothing could be added or omitted to make the effect more pleasing. The clear, unbroken straight lines that frame the *Festsaal* (festival hall) of the Weimar Castle (see picture at left) are contrasted in the small, straight frames of the ceiling patterns. The modest decoration in these small frames is perfectly balanced by the decorations above the columns. The columns themselves are unbroken, straight lines, except for their simple Ionic *capitals* (the scroll decorations at the top). They serve to support the room and to counterbalance the lines of the walls. The smooth, shiny floor reflects the ceiling. The openings between the columns highlight the heavy frieze (ornamental bands) above them. The interruptions of the doors and statues at the end of the room make the simplicity and clarity of the long lines even more elegant. The basic characteristics of the architecture of the interior of the *Festsaal* are also noticeable in the exteriors of churches and public buildings built during this period in many countries. Broad shoulder strips, deep porches supported by massive, formal columns, walls pierced by elegant tall windows and doors, are all part of the classical design.

Festsaal (festival hall), Castle of Weimar (East Germany). Built in 1802 by H. Gentz.

In the painting below, the three swords in the center are balanced by the three curved arches of the background. The three strong sons on the left, with their beautifully proportioned bodies and virile masculinity, are balanced by the three huddled, draped, weeping women on the right. The walls and floor, bare of decoration, are relieved by the geometrical design of their building stones. The central, commanding figure of the father unites the picture, re-emphasizing strength and control. Many classical painters achieved graceful balance by contrasts of similar types. The focal point, like the most important theme in a composition, is often counterbalanced by a second subject of a completely different character, and these materials are highlighted and surrounded by objects of various sizes, colors, textures and designs.

These basic, classical features are expressed in music in simple, flowing, beautiful melodies that move toward predictable cadences (closing chord progressions). Contrasting melodies are used to counterbalance each other. The modest patterning and subtle decoration in classical architecture and painting find musical counterparts in bass configurations such as the *Alberti bass* (see page 18) and elegant but rather sparse ornamentation. The strength of buildings themselves and of central characters in paintings are reflected in strong tonic-dominant harmony. The play of light and shadow finds a correspondence in modulations and sudden accents. The delicate contrasts and reflections of nature can be likened to the *crescendos* and *diminuendos* which add "light and shade" to music. Above all, the perfect balance in all its many styles is most important in music and takes the form of *sonata-allegro* (see page 22). Thus the *sonata-allegro* may be said to turn the basic features of classical design into sound.

Jacques Louis David, *Oath of the Horatii,* 1784. (Toledo Museum of Art.)

The New Classical Performer
from "Co-creator" to "Re-creator"

The development of the pianoforte exerted such a great influence on composers that the style of writing for keyboard slowly changed in many important respects. At Mannheim, in Germany, an orchestra of such great fame that it was called the finest in Europe was unrivaled for its perfection of dynamic shading. Audiences were especially excited and impressed by the gradual *crescendos* and *diminuendos* made by this orchestra under its outstanding conductor, Johann Stamitz.

The new pianoforte also had the expressive capabilities of *crescendo* and *diminuendo.* It could produce delicate shadings of contrasting dynamics, sudden accents, and combine loud and soft sounds at the same time. This enabled the performer to bring out a melodic line, while supporting and accompanying it with a softer, harmonic bass. The bass was the foundation in baroque music, but in classical music, melody assumed primary importance and harmony found new uses.

The pedal which raised the dampers from the strings was a completely new invention. It made further uses of harmonic material possible by its ability to bind together or overlap tones that could not be held with the hands. The *hammer and escapement* mechanism of the piano made another important contribution to musical style. For the first time, a legato melody could be played with changes in volume during its course. In fact, the new action made these legato connections sound so much like singing, that playing "in a singing style" became a necessary attainment for performing in "good taste."

With such an expressive instrument, the addition of ornaments to heighten the expression became less essential, and finally became so "out of taste" as to be condemned. By the end of the classical period, composers began to consider the addition of notes to their compositions unpardonable. The performer was no longer expected to be "co-creator" with the composer. "Good taste" demanded that the composer's written text be faithfully followed, so that the music was "re-created," as nearly as possible, just as the composer conceived it.

Pianoforte built by Robert Stodart, London, 1790. (The Smithsonian Institution.)

Note the elegant, simple, and restrained classical lines, in spite of its resemblance to a baroque harpsichord.

ORNAMENTATION

During the classical era, composers began to follow C.P.E. Bach's suggestion that all ornamentation be written on the page. However, it was many years before performers entirely dropped the custom of adding ornaments, especially in repeated sections, and particularly in slow movements. The same ornament signs which had been devised during the baroque era continued to be used, and the baroque style of performing them continued to be in good taste.

A summary of these ornaments and the acceptable style for playing them will be found below, together with indications of the changes which occurred during the classical era. The performer should use this information for reference in playing all music of the classical era. A more detailed discussion will be found in *THE BAROQUE ERA: An Introduction to the Keyboard Music*, edited by Willard A. Palmer and Margery Halford, published by Alfred.

---

1. THE APPOGGIATURA 

The word *appoggiatura* comes from the Italian "appoggiare," meaning "to lean." The small "leaning note" is played on the beat of the main note. It should be accented and slurred softly into the main note.

C.P.E. Bach suggested that the small note be written in its actual time value. This value is subtracted from the following large note. So great was C.P.E. Bach's influence that almost all composers of the classical period generally followed this practice.

 is played: 

 is played: 

 or  is played: 

 is played: 

 is played: 

Note: The symbol  is simply an old way of writing a sixteenth note  Mozart was among the first to use the symbol with the cross-stroke to indicate a sixteenth-note appoggiatura. It is played *on the beat*, for the value of a sixteenth note.

2. THE TRILL 

Each of the above signs continued to be used to indicate the trill. The trill begins on the upper auxiliary (the next higher scale note). It always begins *on the beat* of its main note, and its speed is adjusted to suit the context of the passage. The following examples serve to show the general configuration of the trill; the number of notes in a trill need not be precisely measured.

 played:  or 

or  or 

 played:  or  or 

or  or  or 

 played:  or 

or  or 

The examples above show the freedom allowed in playing trills. It was also considered especially tasteful to prolong the first note of the trill slightly, before beginning the repercussions.

Many short trills and almost all long trills are played with a *termination* or *suffix* consisting of two notes (the note just below the main note, followed by the main note):

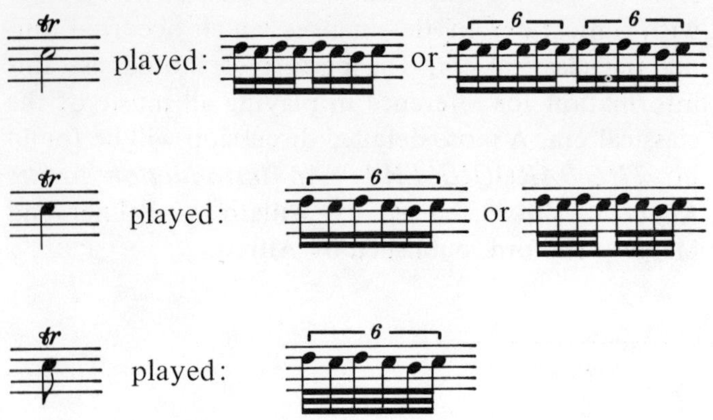

The termination is sometimes written out in notes. The notes of the termination are performed at the same speed as those of the trill:

The trill with termination is especially appropriate when the note following the trill is a whole or half step higher than the main note of the trill. In this case the termination is effective even with short trills.

3. THE APPOGGIATURA & TRILL

In this ornament, the appoggiatura serves as the first note of the trill, which is prolonged for the written value of the appoggiatura, as in example (a), or slightly longer, as in example (b), so that the repercussions begin after the beat, as shown:

4. THE MORDENT

The mordent begins *on the beat* of its main note, descends to the lower auxiliary very quickly, and returns at once to the main note. It adds a brilliant rhythmic accent. During the classical era, the mordent sign was rarely used, since the new pianoforte could produce accents without it.

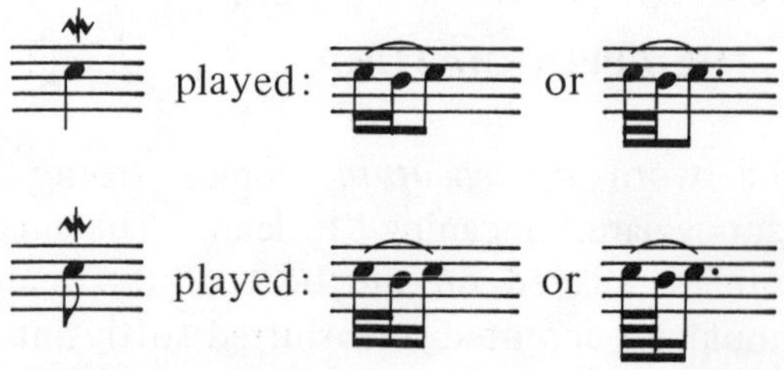

5. THE TURN

When the turn appears *over* the note,

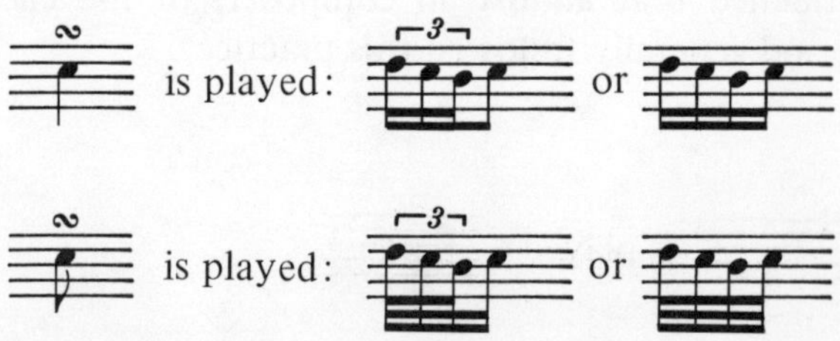

When the turn appears *after* the note, the main note is sounded before the turn is played.

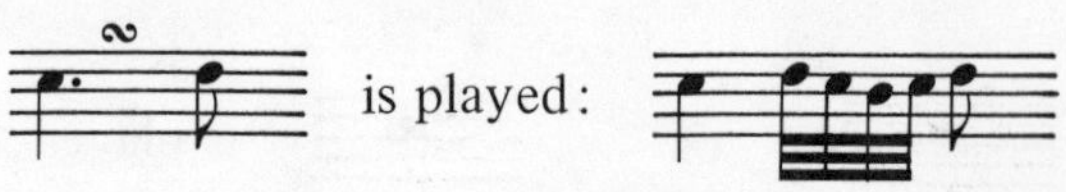

In his *Essay,* C. P. E. Bach remarks that "the turn is almost always performed rapidly."

ACKNOWLEDGMENTS

The editors wish to express their gratitude for the assistance of the many people who have contributed their time, special skills, and painstaking attention to the preparation of this book. Included among these are countless music educators who have encouraged us in our efforts. To the following persons go our special thanks:

To Judith Linder, our brilliant assistant, whose knowledge and expertise are reflected in every facet of the book's preparation. To Iris and Morton Manus, who have contributed an inestimable amount toward making this and other books in the Alfred Masterworks Series publications of the finest quality.

To the department heads and staffs of the libraries which have provided us with microfilms and copies of their priceless source materials, so that this edition may be as accurate as it is possible to make it: the Library of Congress, Washington, D.C.; the British Library, London, England; and the Beethoven-haus, Bonn, Germany.

LEOPOLD MOZART

Leopold Mozart in 1756, the year in which Wolfgang was born.

Leopold Mozart (1719-1787), an important composer of pre-classical music, is chiefly remembered today as the father of the celebrated Wolfgang Amadeus Mozart. He was one of the finest and best-known violinists in Europe, and his textbook entitled *Treatise on the Fundamental Principles of Violin Playing* (1756) is one of the most reliable and comprehensive works on the performance practices of his day. A large section of this book is devoted to instruction in interpreting ornaments and to adding them extemporaneously.

Since Leopold was the teacher of his young children (Wolfgang and his very talented sister, Maria Anna, nicknamed "Nannerl"), it is natural that Wolfgang's earliest compositions are in the same style as his father's. Leopold devoted a considerable part of his life to promoting and educating his children. He wanted all of Europe to appreciate the talents of his son, and he provided Wolfgang with opportunities to hear the music of the greatest composers and performers of his day.

Leopold Mozart with his children Wolfgang and Nannerl in Paris, 1764. Watercolor by Carmontelle.

WOLFGANG AMADEUS MOZART

Wolfgang Amadeus Mozart (1756-1791) was probably the greatest child prodigy in the history of music. Since he began to compose when he was so young, the evolution of the classical style can almost be traced through his compositions. His first works, patterned after those of his father, are light-hearted, elegant, and grew out of the galant style. An awareness of musical form is evident, even in his earliest compositions.

Two of Wolfgang's first works are found on pages 8 - 10, together with editorial suggestions for additional ornamentation. While almost no ornaments appear in the music, these pieces are in the style which requires the performer to add embellishments, especially when sections are repeated.

In spite of his very short life (Mozart lived only to the age of 35), his music spans the classical era, from its beginnings to the time when the classical sonata was a fully developed form and when the classical period was in full flower.

Mozart's music is further discussed later in this book, where an example of one of his more mature compositions is given. A more complete study of Mozart's works is available in the book, *MOZART: An Introduction to his Keyboard Works,* edited by Willard A. Palmer and published by Alfred.

These two menuets, composed by Mozart as a child, are in the *galant* style, showing the influence of his father and teacher, Leopold Mozart. The galant works found in Alfred's *THE BAROQUE ERA* are simply light works in the baroque style. But these pieces by Mozart do not sound baroque at all. The first one begins in the tonic key and ends the A section in the dominant; the B section reverses the procedure. Each section is repeated. This is in the baroque form, and there is still the need for added ornamentation, which has been suggested in light print.

TWO MENUETS
from Sonata in C Major
I

Andante moderato M.M. ♩ = 88-108

Suggested ornamentation for repeat:

Wolfgang Amadeus Mozart

Fine

ⓐ The suggested ornamentation in light print in measures 5 and 13-14 may be reserved for the *da capo*, so that the fullest embellishment of the melody appears in the final hearing.

II

Andante moderato M. M. ♩ = 108 - 116

11
B
14
17
20
D. C. Menuet I

J.S. Bach, whose work culminated the baroque era, gave his children thorough training in all aspects of music. His sons, especially Johann Christian and Carl Philipp Emanuel, became leaders among those who influenced the development of the classical style of music. The strongly national styles of the baroque era were blending together. In the new, highly organized and elegant style, melody became the most important factor, with the remaining parts serving as accompaniment. The newly developed pianoforte allowed combinations of soft and loud at the same time, as well as gradual crescendo and diminuendo. Composers were beginning to indicate exactly where these effects were to be used.

J. C. BACH –"the London Bach"

Johann Christian Bach (1735-1782) was the youngest son of Johann Sebastian Bach. After his father died in 1750, Christian continued his music studies with his older brother, Carl Philipp Emanuel and then went to Rome, where he studied with the famous composer, Padre Martini. There he learned the beautiful singing style that later made him famous as a melodist. He composed and produced operas in the Italian style. In 1762 he went to London to write for the theater. Mozart, only 8 years old but already an accomplished musician, met Christian there in 1764 and was greatly influenced by him. In later years, Mozart said he learned the *cantabile* ("singing") style from Christian Bach.

Christian's music contributed much to the evolution of the classical style, especially the sonata form. Broadly contrasting themes, elegance, restraint, and lyricism, important features of the classical style, are often found in his music.

ENGRAVING BY U. STÖTTRUP

C. P. E. BACH –"the Berlin Bach"

Carl Philipp Emanuel Bach (1714-1788), the second surviving son of Johann Sebastian Bach, became court composer and accompanist to King Frederick the Great, an accomplished flute player, composer, and patron of music. Emanuel spent most of his adult life in Hamburg and Berlin. His compositions for orchestra, church, and chamber groups were very popular, and his expressive playing of his own compositions was particularly famous.

One of Emanuel's greatest contributions to the world of music is the monumental *Essay on the True Art of Keyboard Playing*, published in 1753. This methodical work describes in detail all of his father's principles of performance style, technique, fingering, and ornamentation and is of such importance that Mozart, Haydn, Beethoven, and Clementi found a thorough study of it indispensable. Emanuel advised other musicians to begin writing into the music all the ornaments they wanted played and to write appoggiaturas in their actual note values. In his *Sonatas with Varied Repeats*, he provided examples that followed these precepts.

C. P. E. Bach led the way in the development of the classical sonata. Some of his sonatas have three movements (fast-slow-fast) and use two contrasting themes followed by a development and recapitulation. By writing in idiomatic, sensitive piano style, he influenced the development of piano technic and composition. His notation of ornamentation and dynamics foreshadowed the time when performers were expected to play only what appeared on the page, without improvised additions of their own. Haydn and Mozart, who are generally credited with "ushering in" the classical era, gave this credit to Emanuel Bach.

This selection is an example of the early classical style that grew out of the *rococo* or *galant* music of the baroque period. J. C. Bach, following the advice given by his brother, C. P. E. Bach in his famous *Essay,* has supplied enough ornamentation to make further embellishment by the performer unnecessary.

MINUETTO
from Sonata No. 2 in D Major

Andante moderato M. M. ♩ = 88 - 100

Johann Christian Bach

ⓐ Notice that J.C. Bach wrote the appoggiaturas in the values intended to be played, as recommended in C. P. E. Bach's *Essay.*

ⓑ The wedge-shaped staccato mark (▾) means "release instantly." See the discussion under *Muzio Clementi* on page 45.

Ⓒ The staccato dot (•) indicates a touch slightly less staccato than the wedge (▾). See the discussion under *Muzio Clementi* on page 45.

Minore

38
42
C
45
49
Da Capo il Maggiore
(Repeat the major sections, pp.12-13)

In 1766 Carl Philipp Emanuel Bach published a collection of *Sonatas with Varied Repeats,* from which the following example is taken. The repeats were written out in full rather than indicated by repeat signs. The performer was not expected to add anything. Other composers, including Haydn, Mozart, and Beethoven, followed his example and began to indicate the ornaments they expected performed, and so the tradition of adding embellishments (by the performer) came to an end.

ARIOSO

Carl Philipp Emanuel Bach

ⓐ In measures 4, 8, 12, and 23, C. P. E. Bach uses the "snapped turn" (𝆗) .

This would be performed as follows in measure 4: 

Because the ornament is very difficult at this stage of development, we have used a simple turn, an acceptable substitute.

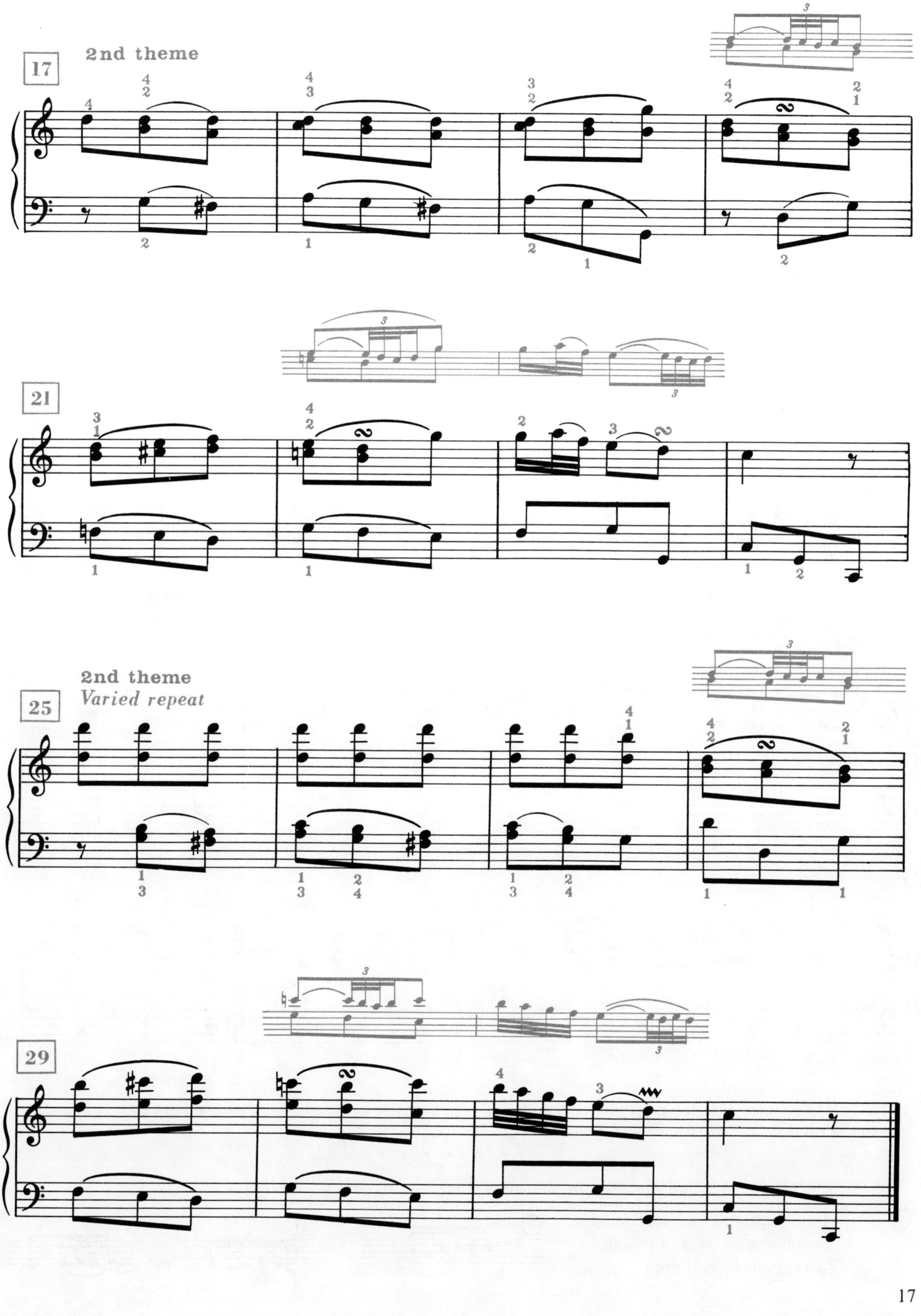
17
2nd theme
21
25
2nd theme
Varied repeat
29

The Italian composer, Domenico Alberti (1710-1740), was very famous during his short lifetime as a singer and harpsichordist. The piece below was written near the end of the baroque era. Alberti did not invent the broken bass figure used in the second variation, but he made use of it in so many compositions that it has been called "Alberti bass." This type of accompaniment is found in the works of virtually all composers of the classical era.

In this piece the performer is expected to add ornaments of his own, particularly when repeating each section (see footnote). The notes in light print in the main text complete the harmony, as was expected in much music of the baroque period.

THEME and VARIATIONS
from Sonata in F

Tempo di minuet

Theme M. M. ♩= 100-120

Domenico Alberti
Op. 1, No. 7

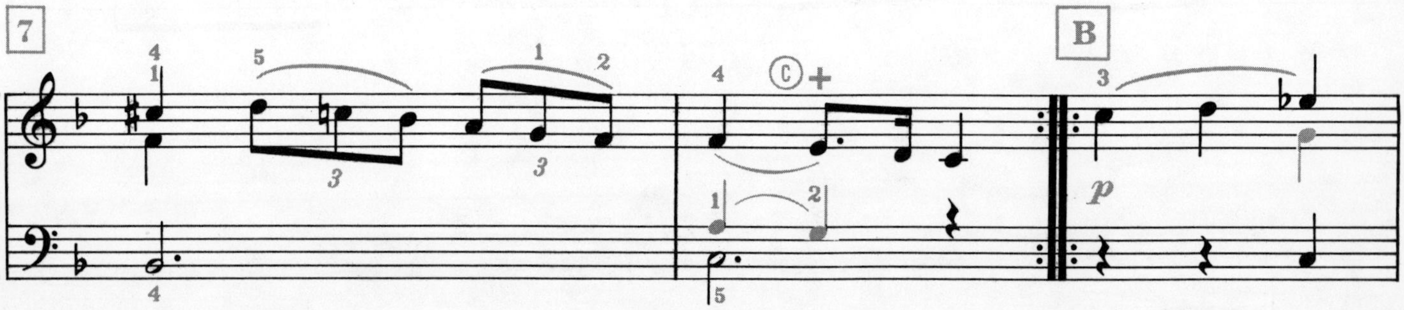

NOTE: It is possible that the pairs of eighth notes and the dotted-eighth/sixteenth pairs should be accommodated to the triplet rhythm in the *theme* and *variation 1*:

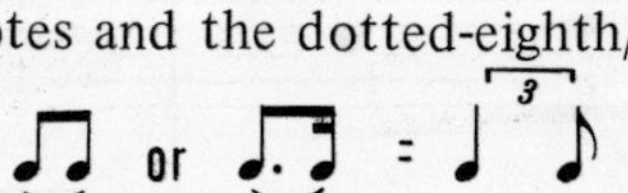

This practice was common in the baroque period. See Alfred's *THE BAROQUE ERA*.

ⓐ ⓑ ⓒ Upon repeating each section a trill may be added where a plus sign (+) appears in light print:

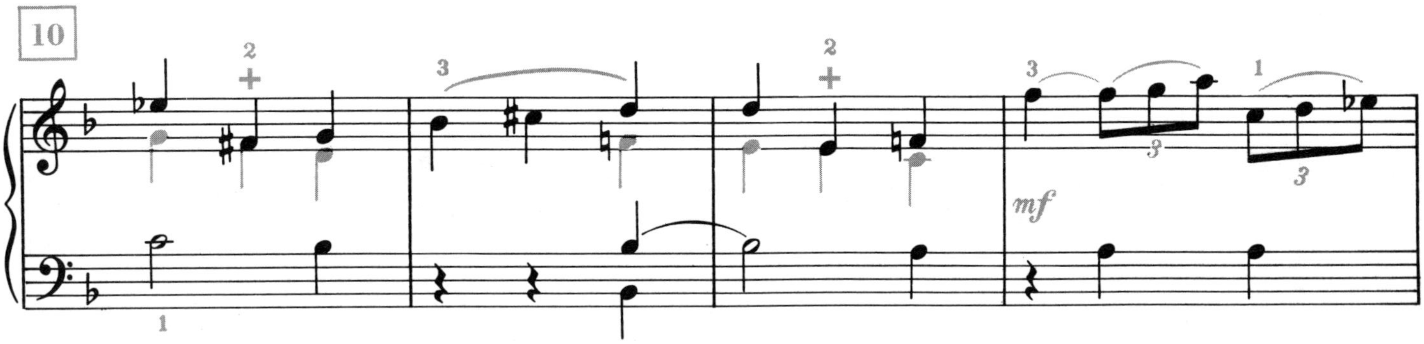

ⓓ The editors believe that this measure should be played exactly the same as measure 8. This is possibly an example of the casual notation used by most composers of the baroque period. This is discussed in *THE BAROQUE ERA*.

Variation 2

ⓔ This notation is probably more correct. See footnote ⓓ on page 19.

The Classical Sonata

The word *sonata* was first used simply to indicate a piece to be played instead of a piece to be sung (*cantata*). Most baroque sonatas consisted of one movement in binary (two part) form. The first section began in the tonic key and modulated so that it ended in the dominant; the second section began in the dominant and modulated so as to end in the tonic. Each section was repeated. Some baroque sonatas had as many as five movements, generally all in the same key. Contrast was provided by different tempos for each movement. Each movement was constructed principally from one motive and generally contained no contrasting thematic material.

As the ideals of the classical era became widespread, the balance, contrast, symmetry, restraint, etc., so noticeable in architecture and art became reflected in music, particularly in the development of the form known as the *classical sonata.*

The first movement of a classical sonata is usually an *allegro* movement and ideally follows a symmetrical form that came to be known as *sonata-allegro.* This form is used for the first movement of the keyboard sonata, the concerto (sonata for solo instrument and orchestra), the symphony (sonata for orchestra), the quartet or quintet, and the sonata for small instrumental ensemble.

This form differs from the baroque sonata principally because two contrasting themes are used, the first in the tonic and the second in the dominant. This first section is called the EXPOSITION or "exposing" of the principal themes. The beginning of the second section, called the DEVELOPMENT, is a new ingredient, a section in which the composer is expected to show skill and artistry in his imaginative handling of the themes introduced in the first section. After this, in the RECAPITULATION, the themes are restated, both in the tonic.

A SUMMARY OF SONATA-ALLEGRO FORM

A — EXPOSITION

- introductory measures (optional)
- *1st theme:* tonic key, modulation to dominant key*
- *2nd theme*: dominant key*
- usually a short closing section (*coda* or *codetta*), ending in the dominant key*

B — DEVELOPMENT

- begins in dominant key, ends in tonic; may modulate in-between to any desired key or keys

  (composer is free to use his imagination and compositional skills in developing the thematic material)
- modulation back to tonic key

A — RECAPITULATION

- *1st theme* restated in the tonic key
- *2nd theme* restated in the tonic key
- closing *coda* or *codetta* of any length to provide a satisfactory tonic ending

*The modulations are to the dominant key if the sonata is in a major key. Very often, if it is in a minor key, the modulations are to the relative major, instead.

This form is very flexible, as will be noted in the examples on the following pages. In the recapitulation, for example, themes may be restated with small alterations. Sometimes a third theme may be introduced in the exposition, etc.

The classical sonata usually has 3 or 4 movements. The first is usually in *sonata-allegro* form. The second is usually slow, highly expressive, and very often in simple A B A form. If there are 4 movements, the 3rd is a dance: usually a *minuet & trio* or *scherzo.* The final movement may be a *rondo,* a *theme & variations,* or *sonata-allegro* form.

The key relationship between movements is essential. The first and last movements must begin and end in the tonic key. The second movement may be in the relative major (or minor) key, or in the key of the dominant or sub-dominant. It must, however, be in a key related to the first movement. Each movement has its own identifiable themes.

Georg Christoph Wagenseil (1715-1777) was a court composer and music master to the Empress Maria Theresa of Austria. His compositions were evidently quite popular, for Mozart, at age 6, performed one of his concertos for the court and asked particularly for Wagenseil to turn pages for him.

A *sonatina* is a very short *sonata*. This movement meets all the requirements of *sonata-allegro* form, even though each section is very brief. In many sonatinas the development section serves only as a transition from the dominant back to the tonic. Occasionally one or more parts of a sonata-allegro movement may be missing. This piece is probably one of the shortest examples of the form in which all of its elements are present.

SONATINA IN C
(1st Movement)

Georg Christoph Wagenseil

ⓐ Notice that Wagenseil writes the appoggiaturas in their actual time values.

ⓑ **DEVELOPMENT**

RECAPITULATION

1st Theme (TONIC)

2nd Theme (TONIC)

CODETTA (TONIC)

ⓑ In a *sonatina* the development section may be missing altogether. Here it serves principally as a modulation back to the tonic, in preparation for the recapitulation. The 1st theme is developed only to the extent that the 1st measure is inverted.

FRANZ JOSEPH HAYDN

Franz Joseph Haydn (1732-1809), like so many of the great master composers, showed exceptional musical talent when he was a young child. Beginning at age 5, he was given instructions in singing, violin, keyboard playing, as well as other instruments. As a composer he was largely self-taught, and his chief sources of study included the keyboard sonatas of C.P.E. Bach. Haydn once said, "Whoever knows me thoroughly must discover that I owe a great deal to Emanuel Bach, that I understood him and studied him diligently. Emanuel Bach once complimented me on this fact himself."

Haydn in 1792. Painting by Thomas Hardy.

During the years 1761-1790, Haydn was in the service of Prince Esterházy, one of the wealthiest Hungarian noblemen. Haydn became the supreme example of the royal court musician and composer, with an orchestra of 25 well-trained, devoted musicians to try all his ideas. He was also the organizer, coach, and conductor for all operatic presentations in the royal palace. It was modeled after the court of Versailles, a magnificent edifice with two theaters.

Haydn's works illustrate the great flexibility of the structure of sonata-allegro form. He shows great ingenuity in making subtle changes that enhance without changing the large outline. It is often noted that many of his sonata-allegro movements are constructed on only one theme. The same might be said for the first movement of the sonata beginning on page 28. It should be pointed out that, although the basic motive upon which the second theme is built is the same as that of the first theme, it is presented in the exposition in the dominant and returns in the recapitulation in the tonic. Thus, it serves the function of a second theme.

Haydn leads his string quartet in a rehearsal at the Esterházy castle.

Besides the monumental oratorios, *The Seasons* and *The Creation,* Haydn composed operas, songs, theater music, 104 symphonies, 60 keyboard sonatas, and much chamber music. Few composers have been as highly respected and revered in their own lifetime as Haydn.

When Haydn visited England, he was given a great welcome by royalty and by the public. There he heard a performance of Handel's *Messiah* and was so inspired that he wrote *The Creation* shortly thereafter. He was awarded an honorary doctorate by Cambridge University. A more complete study of Haydn's works is available in the book, *HAYDN: An Introduction to his Keyboard Works,* edited by George Lucktenberg and published by Alfred.

In this piece Haydn shows the influence of C.P.E. Bach in that he does not depend on the performer to provide variants when the theme is repeated, but writes them out in full. Compare with the *Arioso* on pages 16-17. Bach's piece uses two themes, Haydn's only one.

AIR

Innocentemente M. M. ♩ = 88 - 96 **Franz Joseph Haydn**

Theme

Theme
Varied by using Alberti bass

ⓐ The wedge-shaped staccato marks (▼) do not imply any particular stress or emphasis. In music of this period they simply mean that the note is to be released instantly. See *CLEMENTI'S RULES FOR STACCATO* at the bottom of page 45.

ⓑ This note should be played shorter than its notated value, as shown in the small staff. This was the practice with short notes of anticipation, particularly when preceded by a trill.

Theme
Varied by using double notes and L.H. trill-like figures

This sonata consists of 3 movements:

1. Sonata-allegro form (abbreviated, or *sonatina* form).
2. Menuet & Trio
3. Sonata-allegro form.

Note that the term *sonata-allegro* is used for the first and last movements in spite of their respective tempo indications, *Moderato* and *Presto*.

As you follow the analysis of the forms, indicated in light print, note how Haydn adheres to the basic forms, at the same time allowing himself considerable flexibility.

SONATA IN C
(1st Movement)

Moderato M. M. ♩= 66-69

Franz Joseph Haydn

Ⓐ There should be no perceptible break between the last note of the slur and the following note. The purpose of the slur is to show legato connection between the slurred notes, and a slight stress or emphasis on the note following the slur. Such markings are derived from bowing indications for stringed instruments.

Ⓑ The 2nd theme is constructed from the same motive as the 1st theme, but the motive is dealt with in a contrasting manner. This would seem at first glance to be simply a continuation of the 1st theme, but it appears here in the *dominant*, and in the recapitulation in the *tonic*. Thus it serves the purpose of a 2nd theme in this abbreviated *sonata-allegro (sonatina)* form.

ⓒ This realization of the *turn,* using "overdotting," is easier to play and more pleasing to the ear than a realization that sticks very strictly to the indicated rhythm: 

See footnote ⓑ on page 26.

ⓓ A *turn*  may be substituted for the *trill.*

DEVELOPMENT

ⓔ A *turn* may be substituted for the *trill*.

(2nd Movement)

Menuet M. M. ♩ = 112-120

TRIO

Menuet da Capo

ⓐ A rule given by C. P. E. Bach and J. J. Quantz states that, when a note is followed by a rest, its appoggiatura (small note) may receive the value of the large note, and the large note the value of the rest. This seems applicable here, particularly since Haydn indicated the small note as a quarter note.

(3rd Movement)

Finale

ⓐ **Presto** M.M. ♩= 100-104

ⓐ Although the tempo is *Presto,* the form of this movement is still termed *sonata-allegro.*

ⓑ These measures (from here to the coda) function as a digression into the key of G minor, the parallel minor of the *dominant* key (G Major). They serve to fill out the movement and provide contrast through use of the minor mode.

37
DEVELOPMENT
f
41
45
cresc.
49
dim.
poco
a-
53
poco
p

RECAPITULATION
1st Theme (TONIC)
2nd Theme
(TONIC)
cresc.

ⓒ These measures correspond to those mentioned in footnote ⓑ on page 35. Since here they are part of the recapitulation, they are stated in the key of the *tonic* minor.

WOLFGANG AMADEUS MOZART

Mozart at 27
Unfinished oil painting by Joseph Lange
(Stiftung Mozarteum, Salzburg)

The composer most admired by Haydn was Wolfgang Amadeus Mozart (1756-1791). Haydn told Mozart's father, "I tell you before God and as an honest man that your son is the greatest composer I know personally or by reputation. He has taste and, apart from that, the greatest possible knowledge of composition." Mozart met Haydn in Vienna in the winter of 1781-82. While Mozart had been greatly influenced by Haydn's development of the sonata structure, Haydn was also influenced by the more mature works of Mozart, and freely admitted it.

Mozart first learned the Italian *cantabile* style in London at the age of 8 under the influence of Johann Christian Bach. Later in Italy, when he was 13, he studied with Christian Bach's teacher, Padre Martini. Mozart's composing was also heavily influenced by the works of Carl Philipp Emanuel Bach, of whom he said, "He is the father, we are the children. Anything we do correctly we learned from him, and anyone who does not admit it is a scoundrel."

Pianoforte by Johann Andreas Stein (1773)

The expressive possibilities of the pianoforte delighted Mozart. When he first played on the excellent instruments built by Stein in 1777, he was enchanted by the effectiveness of the damper pedal. He also realized that the *escapement,* which allowed the hammers to rebound instantly from the strings, opened up new possibilities for legato playing. Although during the days of Mozart and Haydn the ordinary manner of playing was a detached style, legato was to be desired, especially in slow movements. This fact was emphasized by C.P.E. Bach in his famous *Essay.*

Mozart's music is filled with the newly developed dynamic signs and sudden accents, crescendos, and diminuendos. It combines the flowing melodies of the Italian school, the expressiveness and "soul" of the French, and the discipline and sensitivity of the new German style.

This selection is known to pianists as the first movement of *Viennese Sonatina No. 1.* In its original form it is the first movement of *Divertimento IV* for two clarinets (or bassett horns) and bassoon, or 3 bassett horns. Composed in 1783 in Vienna, it represents one of Mozart's more mature works. It is not known who first made the piano transcriptions of the *Divertimenti* and called them the "Viennese Sonatinas," but some of them were published in the early 1800s by Artaria in Vienna.

This movement is particularly effective as a piano piece. It is in true *sonata-allegro* form and shows how the sonata form was used for instruments other than the piano, as well as for pieces with titles other than *sonata.*

The six "Viennese Sonatinas" are available in an edition by Willard A. Palmer, published by Alfred.

DIVERTIMENTO
"Viennese Sonatina," No. 1

Allegro M. M. ♩= 132-144

W. A. Mozart
transcribed and edited
by Willard A. Palmer

2nd Theme
IN G MAJOR
(THE DOMINANT)

DEVELOPMENT

RECAPITULATION

1st Theme

(TONIC)

45 ⓐ

49

53

57

ⓐ The first transcriber of the "Viennese Sonatinas" omitted measures 45-59, and modern editors have done the same without consulting Mozart's original version. This destroys the form of the movement by eliminating the return of the 1st theme in the recapitulation.

60 2nd Theme
(TONIC)
63
67
CODA
(TONIC)
sf
p
71
cresc.
75
f

MUZIO CLEMENTI & the "Legato School"

Muzio Clementi (1752-1832), Italian by birth, lived in England the greater part of his life and considered himself an Englishman. He made such outstanding contributions to piano playing that he is considered to be the founder of the modern school of piano technic. His methods are clearly expressed in the *Introduction to the Art of Playing on the Pianoforte,* which he published around 1803. It enjoyed unprecedented popularity, appearing in eleven different editions. His ideas of composition, performance style, fingering, and ornamentation were formulated from a thorough study of C.P.E. Bach's *Essay on the True Art of Keyboard Playing.* Clementi said, "Whatever I understand of fingering and the new style. . . and of the pianoforte I learned from this book."

Muzio Clementi in 1794. Engraving by T. Hardy

Nevertheless, with Clementi the "ordinary way of playing" began to change from the detached style (described in C.P.E. Bach's *Essay*) to legato. In his method book, Clementi wrote, "when the composer leaves the LEGATO and STACCATO to the performer's taste; let the LEGATO prevail; reserving the STACCATO to give SPIRIT occasionally to set off the HIGHER BEAUTIES of the LEGATO." In his later years, Clementi told one of his pupils that "the more melodic and truly noble style of performance became possible because of the perfection of the piano mechanism." He believed that in Mozart's time, "faulty construction stood in the way of a cantabile and legato style of playing."

Clementi adopted the baroque use of ornaments, following the principles contained in C.P.E. Bach's *Essay.* The only exception he allowed (although his fingerings indicate that he almost never used it himself) was that trills in a legato melody and short trills on passing notes could begin on the principal note instead of the upper auxiliary. "This," he said, "is left chiefly to the taste of the performer."

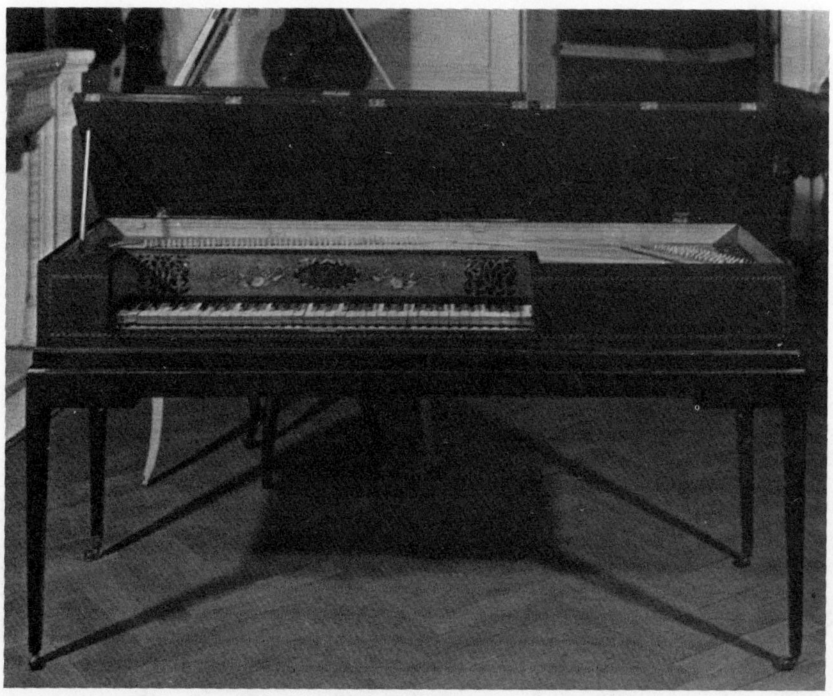

Square pianoforte made by Clementi, c. 1810

Not only successful as a pianist, composer, and teacher, Clementi prospered as a music publisher and as a manufacturer of fine pianos. He lived a long life, wealthy and highly esteemed by his contemporaries.

CLEMENTI'S RULES FOR STACCATO

Wedges: Lift the finger as soon as it has struck the key.

Dots: Less staccato than the wedge.

Dots under a slur: Still less staccato.

This version of the first movement of Clementi's *Sonatina,* Opus 36, No. 6, is from his 6th edition of the *Sonatinas,* which Clementi himself published in 1820. This is his final version, which he says contains "considerable improvements by the author." It makes use of the extended range of the pianoforte and is in many other respects more interesting than the early form of the piece.

Remember that in this piece all notes not marked staccato are played legato. This custom began with Clementi and Beethoven, and the "long legato line" was used even in allegro movements. The first legato phrase extends from the beginning note to the eighth rest in the 2nd full measure. The slur in the 2nd measure simply warns against breaking the phrase after the highest note, A.

The fingering in dark print is Clementi's own. Additional fingering has been added in light print by the editors. Where two sets of fingering are given, the performer may choose whichever is preferred.

SONATINA IN D
(1st Movement)

Allegro con spirito M. M. ♩ = 116-126

EXPOSITION
1st Theme
IN D MAJOR (TONIC)

Muzio Clementi
Op. 36, No. 6

ⓐ Clementi's indication, *mezzo,* probably implies *mezzo forte.*

2nd Theme
IN A MAJOR
(DOMINANT)

24
fz
27
CODA
(DOMINANT)
30
8va
ff
33
loco
p
36
cresc.
f

ⓑ EPISODE

ⓑ Although this is the *development section* of the *sonata-allegro* form, we have termed it *"episode"* since it contains new material rather than an elaboration of previous material. It answers one of the purposes of a development section, however, in that it begins in the dominant and modulates to the tonic, thus serving as a "retransition" to the original key. This is an example of the flexibility allowed within the framework of sonata-allegro form, particularly in a sonatina.

Ⓒ At fermatas such as this, it was customary for the performer to improvise a cadenza such as the following one:

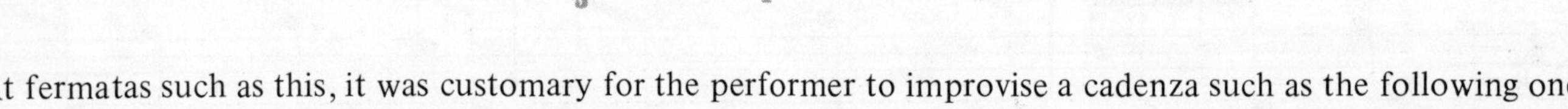

Ⓓ The modern piano has considerably more resonance than Clementi's, so his pedal indication (in dark print) is not appropriate. The performer may pedal again as the suggestions in light print suggest.

68
8va
loco
f
70
ff
fz
fz
73
fz
75
2nd Theme
(TONIC)
dolce
78
fz

81
84
CODA
(TONIC)
86
88
8va
p
90
loco
cresc.
f

LUDWIG VAN BEETHOVEN

Beethoven (1770-1827) was born when musical classicism was in full force in the music of Haydn and Mozart. At that time, the 14 year old Mozart was making his first tours of Italy, and Haydn had already served 10 years as court musician for Prince Esterházy. The 18 year old Clementi was a sensation in London as a concert pianist. Beethoven has been called the "greatest musical imagination of the age." He culminates the accomplishments of the classical era.

BEETHOVEN
From the oil portrait by W. J. Mahler (1804)
(Historisches Museum der Stadt Wien)

Beethoven recommended C.P.E. Bach's *Essay* as well as Clementi's piano method to his own students. He admired the compositions of Haydn and Mozart. He played for Mozart, who predicted a brilliant future for him. He studied briefly with Haydn and also with Neefe, Salieri, and Albrechtsberger, all very famous musicians of their time.

By the time Beethoven was 30, he was one of the most renowned pianists and composers in Europe. It was partly due to his urging that the piano was greatly strengthened, so that the volume and resonance were much increased. Each of his new compositions was a sensation, and Beethoven's name was known to every musician in Europe and England. All who visited Vienna, where Beethoven spent most of his adult life, wanted to meet the great man, even though his deafness finally made him a recluse.

Although he adhered to classical forms, Beethoven's music was highly innovative from the beginning. Even his first symphony, modeled on Haydn's works, is characteristically filled with new ideas, beginning even with the first chord, which to 18th-century ears was highly dissonant. With the "Eroica" symphony in 1803, Beethoven began to use the classical forms in a more romantic fashion. For this reason, his later work will be found in Alfred's *THE ROMANTIC ERA: An Introduction to the Piano Works.* Among his innovations was the use of 3 and even 4 themes in the *sonata-allegro* and the merging of the bridge or transition passage with the thematic material so that a specific point of transition often cannot be identified. In the development section, themes are revealed often with new meanings and in the recapitulation, they are heard again, but from a new viewpoint evolved in the development, instead of simply being repeated as originally heard. In these and other ways, the highly flexible classical sonata was used as the pattern upon which many great romantic works were to be created.

One of Beethoven's pianos, made by Sebastian Erard of Paris.
This instrument was presented to Beethoven in 1803.

Beethoven, like Clementi, adopted the legato style as the basic touch for keyboard playing, indicating detached notes with wedges, dots, and dots under slurs (see the note at the bottom of page 45). A more detailed study of Beethoven's works is available in the book, *BEETHOVEN: An Introduction to his Piano Works,* edited by Willard A. Palmer and published by Alfred.

This *Bagatelle,* composed in 1782, is evidence that Beethoven, even at the age of 12, was influenced by C.P.E. Bach. The material is stated in simple A B A form on this page. After a brief development section (measures 21-30, closing with an opitional cadenza), measures 1-20 are presented again, this time with the repeats written out in full and varied in the style of C.P.E. Bach's *Sonatas with Varied Repeats.*

BAGATELLE

ⓐ **Allegretto quasi andante** M. M. ♩= 69-76
con una certa expressione parlante

Ludwig van Beethoven
Op. 33, No. 6

ⓐ "Allegretto, almost like Andante, with a certain declamatory (speech-like) expression."

ⓑ The wedge-shaped staccato marks (▾) do not imply any special stress or emphasis on the note. Simply release the note instantly. See *CLEMENTI'S RULES FOR STACCATO on page 45.*

Ⓒ At fermatas such as this, it was customary for the performer to improvise a cadenza.

Suggested cadenza for this measure:

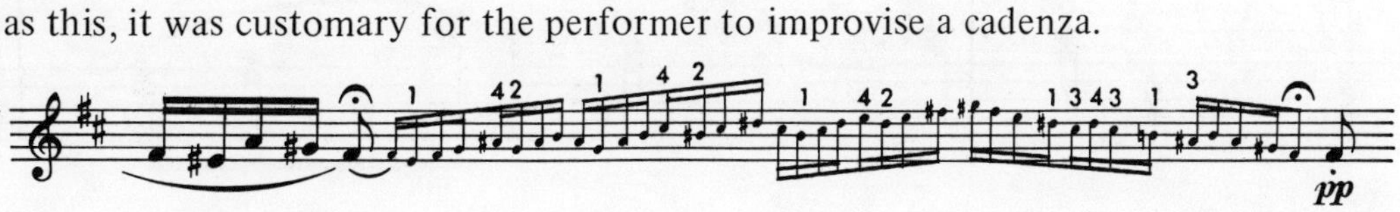

43
47
B
A
Theme
cresc.
sf
p
52
57
Varied repeat of
previous 12 measures
61

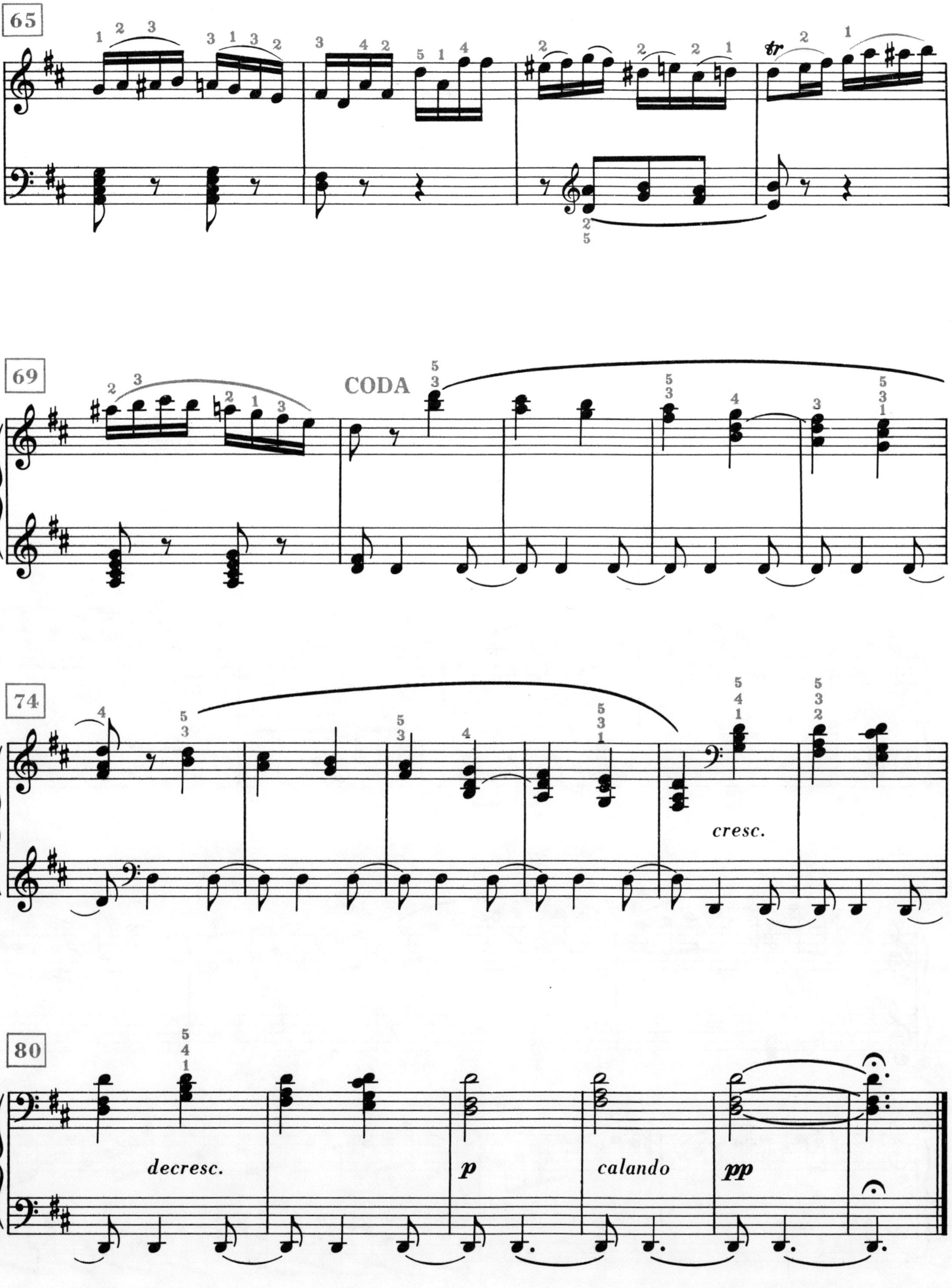
65
69
CODA
74
cresc.
80
decresc.
p
calando
pp

In spite of its opus number, this piece is an early work (around 1796). This movement is interesting because it adheres closely to sonata-allegro form but, at the same time, introduces an extension section into the exposition, development, and recapitulation which can almost be considered a third theme. Beethoven, characteristically unpredictable, begins the development in the key of D Minor rather than D Major. However, this was not a new device. It was used by Haydn in some of his earliest keyboard sonatas.

SONATA IN G

(1st Movement)

Allegro ma non troppo M. M. ♩ = 116-120

Ludwig van Beethoven
Op. 49, No. 2

EXPOSITION
1st Theme
IN G MAJOR (THE TONIC)

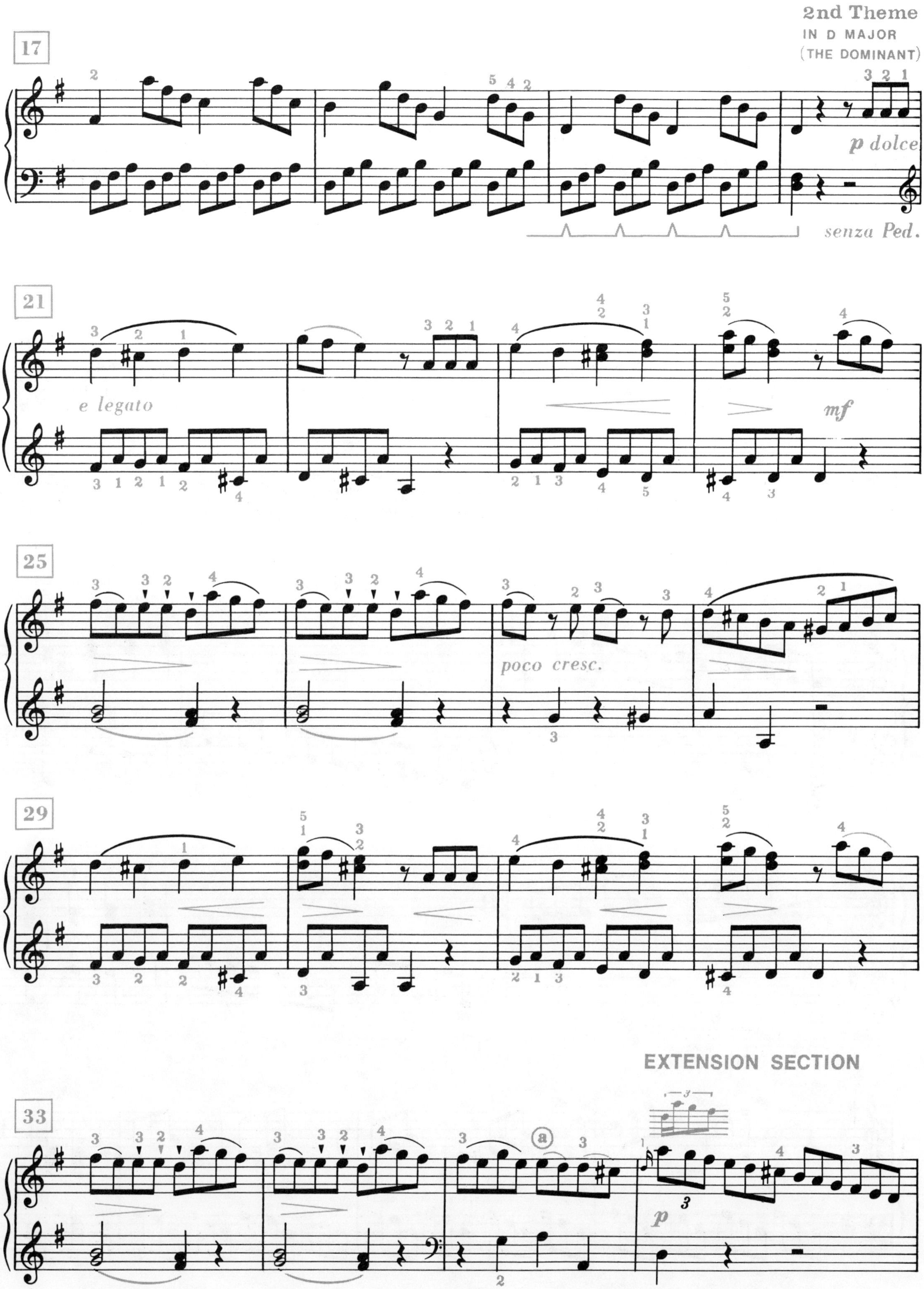

ⓐ In the original edition, the slur here included all four eighth notes, but see the parallel passage at measure 102.

37
poco cresc.
Ped. simile
40
poco dim.
43
46
49
CODETTA
mf
p
dim.
pp

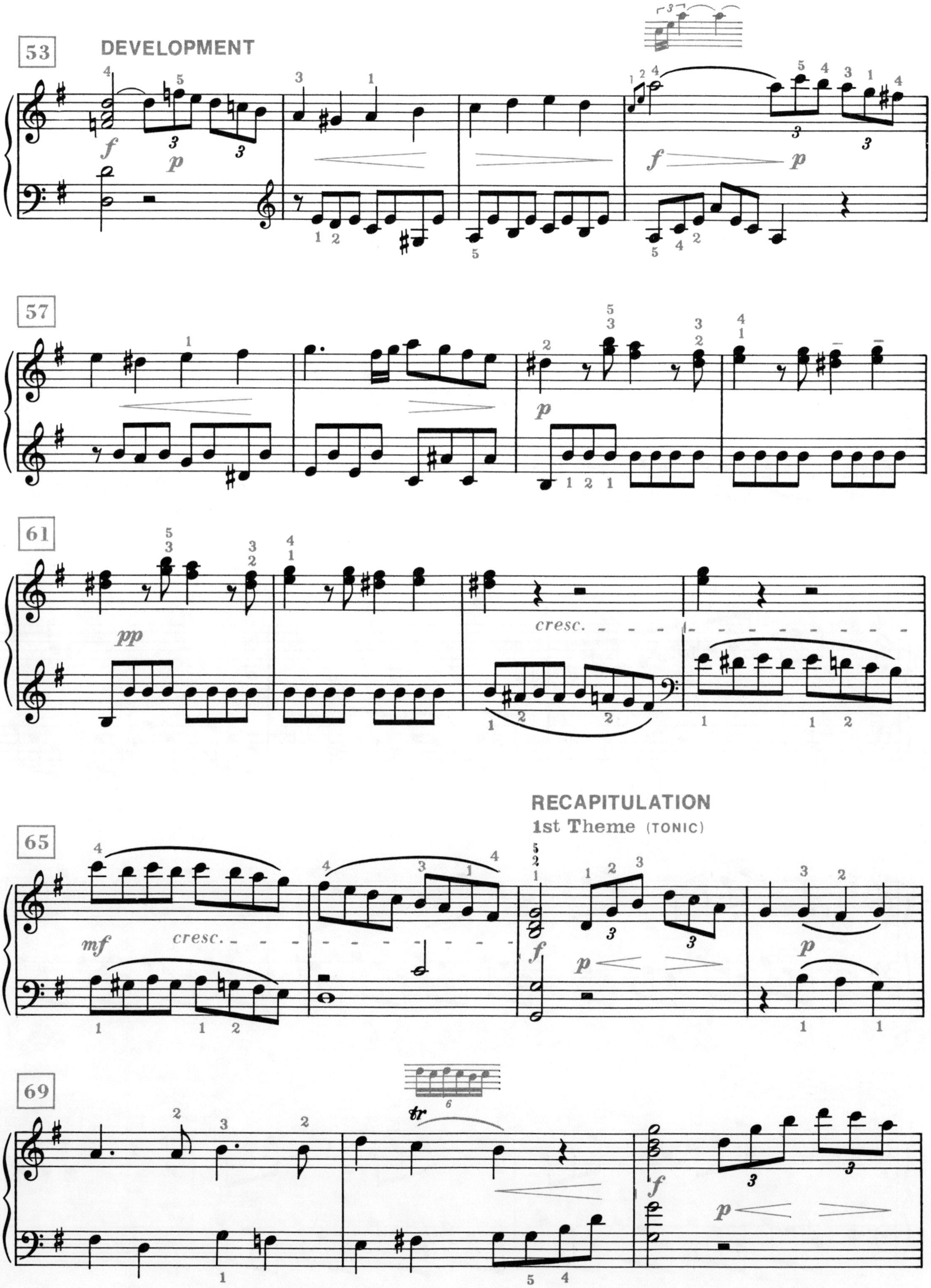
53
DEVELOPMENT
57
61
cresc.
RECAPITULATION
1st Theme (TONIC)
65
cresc.
69

EXTENSION SECTION

EXTENSION SECTION

ⓑ In the original edition, in measures 92-93, the slurs include also the preceding note (G), probably an engraver's error. See the parallel passages at measures 25-26, 33-34, and 100-101.

106
mf
Ped. simile
dim.
109
112
115
legato mf
p
mf
Ped. simile
119
p
cresc.
f